Cousins in the Countryside

Hawys Morgan

Illustrated by Amy Willcox

Schofield & Sims

It's the youth club end of term trip to the countryside.

Lou and Yousef are cousins. Lou is younger than Yousef.

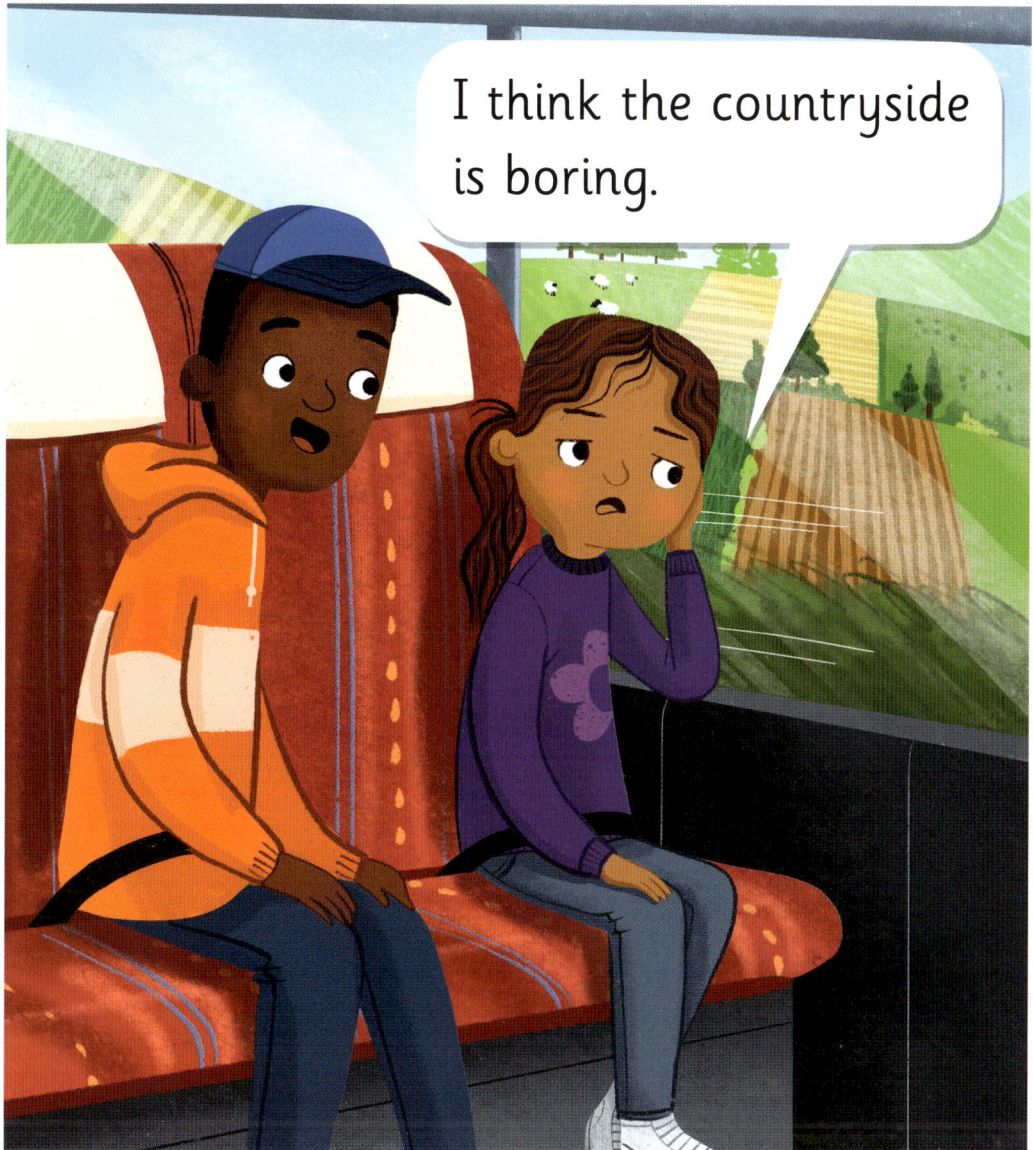

I think the countryside is boring.

Doug leads their group. First, they try the low ropes.

Lou is too young for the high ropes.
She feels cross that she is too little.

Next, Lou and Yousef fly down the zip wire.

Yousef is much bigger than Lou, so he goes quicker than her.

They stand in a row to do archery.

string

target

bow

arrow

1. Put the arrow on the bow.

2. Pull back the string to your shoulder.

3. Let go.

✓ Aim at the target.

✗ Don't shoot in the air.

4. You did it!

It's time to try bouldering.

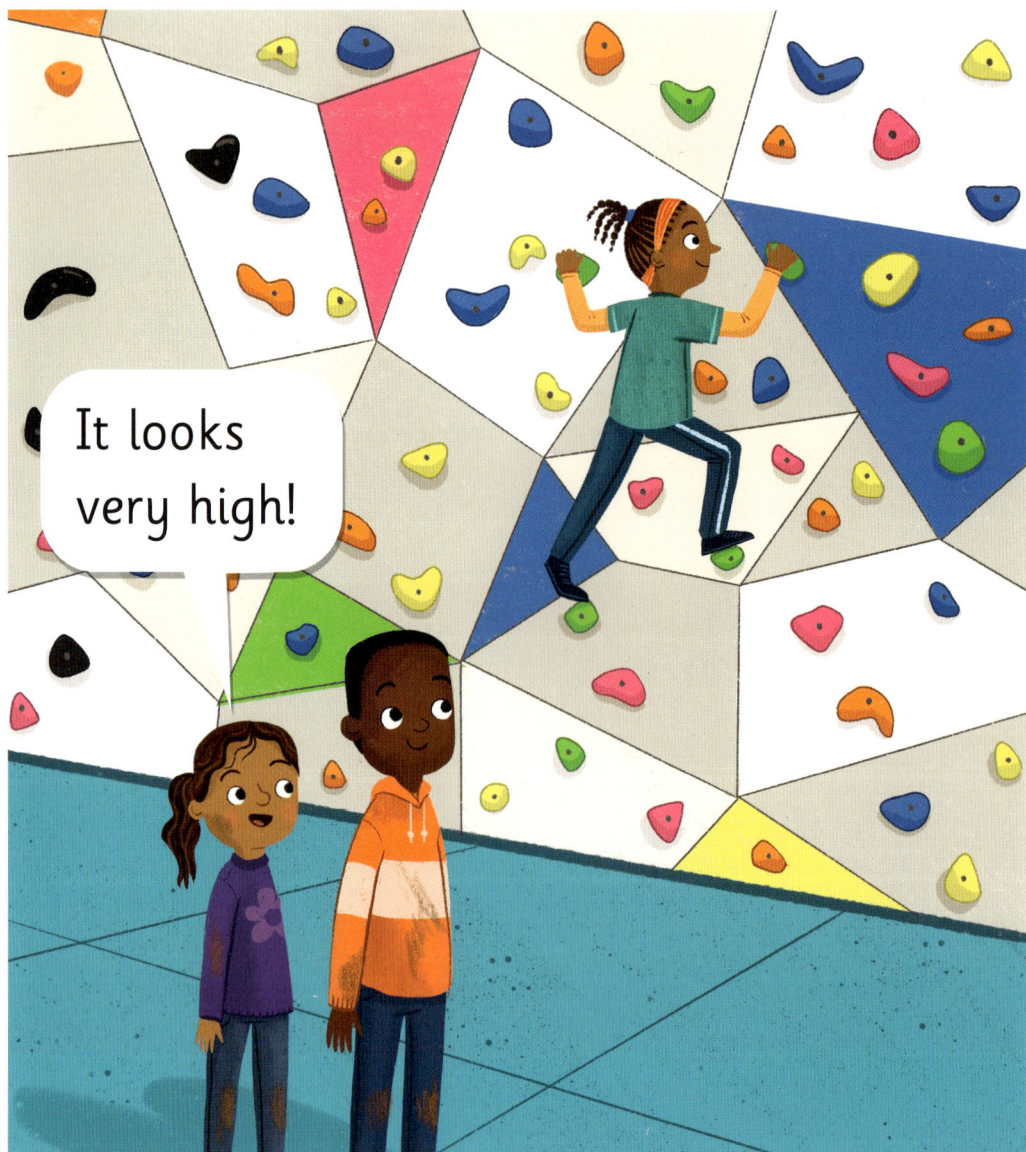

It looks very high!

Lou and Yousef take different ways up. Lou gets to the top first!

Then Doug hands them a map.

Use this map to find the lake.

This glows in the dark so you can see it at night.

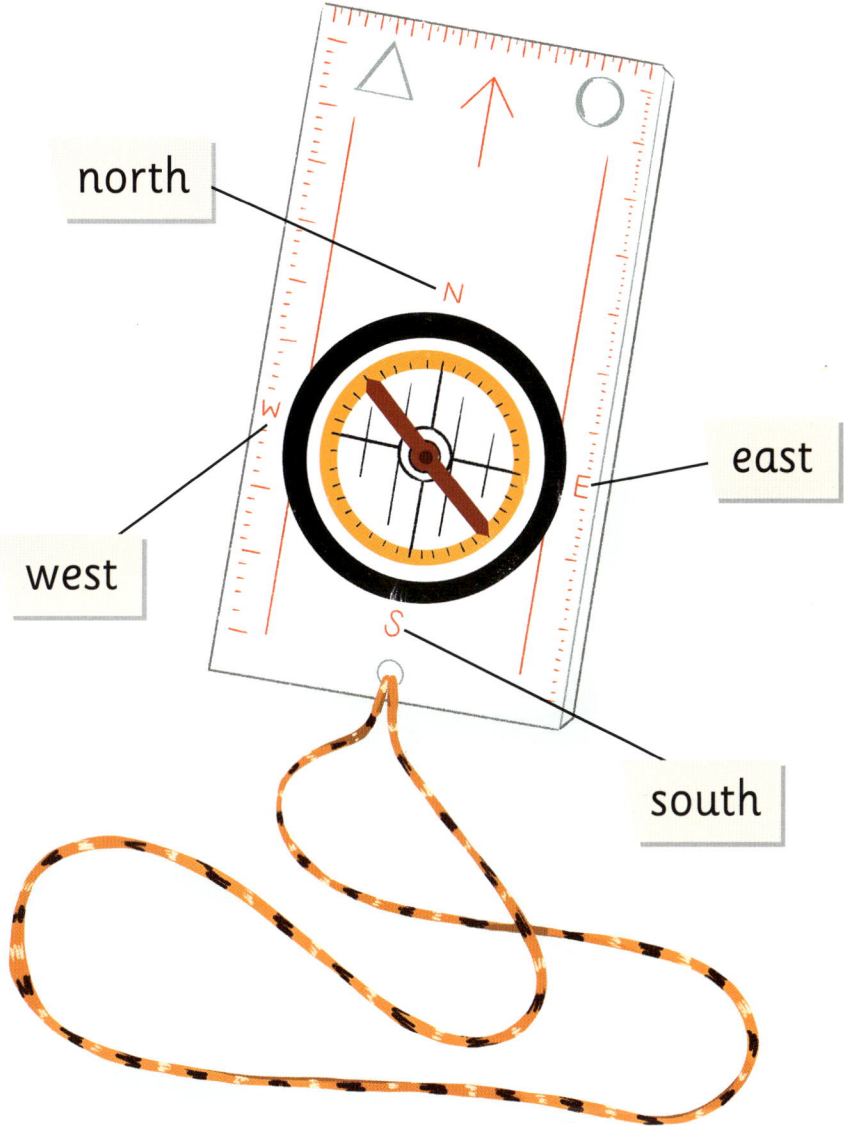

north

N

east

E

west

W

south

S

When they reach the lake, Doug begins to make a fire.
Yousef asks, "How do you light a campfire?"

1. Find dry sticks.

2. Dig a fire pit.

3. Put stones around the pit.

4. Blow softly on the flame.

Doug heats soup on the smouldering fire.

They eat their bowls of soup with some chunks of bread.

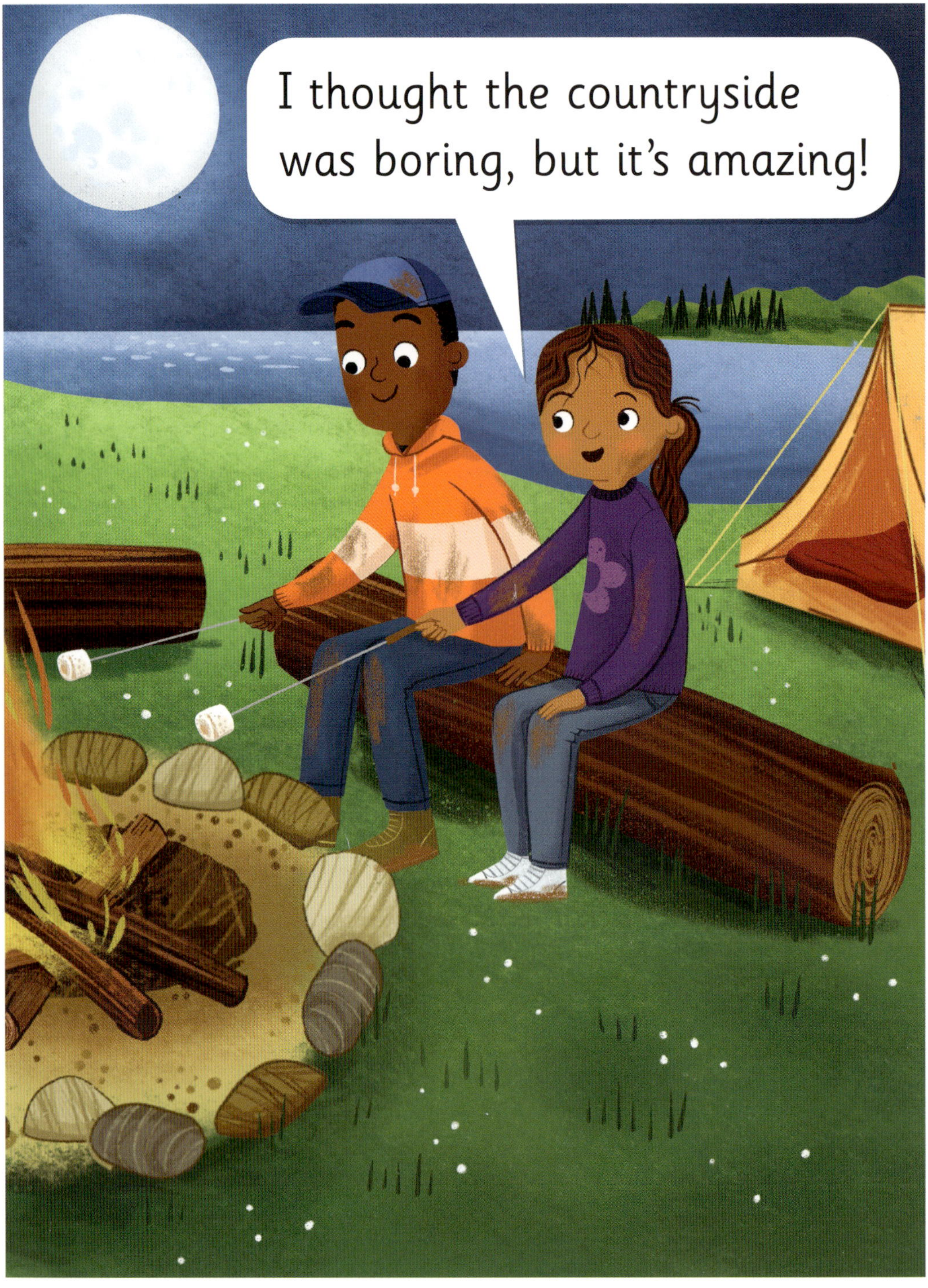
I thought the countryside was boring, but it's amazing!